March 21, 1977

Kahlil Gibran
The Spirit of Friendship

Kahlil Gibran
THE SPIRIT
OF FRIENDSHIP

Illustrated by David Johnston

Hallmark Crown Editions

Selected by Aileene Herrbach Neighbors

Kahlil Gibran

The Spirit of Friendship

KAHLIL GIBRAN

No voice has ever roared from the top of the snowy
mountains of the land of the cedars and been heard in
the Western world as has that of Kahlil Gibran, the
Lebanese poet-philosopher....In his romantic writings,
Gibran tries to unravel the mystery of love while
acknowledging that the more he tries to understand love
the more it becomes mysterious to him....The overall
thrill which he gives to his readers is a mixture of Oriental
sensitivity and Western analytical thinking.

Kahlil Gibran was born in 1883 at the village of
Bsharreh in Mount Lebanon, perched over 3000 feet above
sea level. Gibran had to face a rugged physical environment
and a culture dominated by old and rigid customs by which
the individual is trained to treat the past as his only guide
for the future. He must continue the sacred traditions
and customs woven by a rigid patriarchal society forcing
its members to toe the line in thought and behavior. The
young Kahlil learned Arabic, Syriac (which was then a

moribund language), the catechism and the Psalms of David. His mother, who seems to have been an exceptionally well-read woman, was fond of reading to him tales of Antar, El-Zir, Abu Nuwas and Harun El Rashid....

When life in Lebanon became very hard, the Gibrans, like many other families, emigrated to the United States to find a better living. The young Kahlil was sent to a public school, and it was there, incidentally, that the spelling of his name was changed from Khalil, meaning "friend," to Kahlil, as it was hard for his American classmates to pronounce his name. In his late teens his mother sent him back to Lebanon.... Back in Beirut, the young Gibran continued his college studies, even editing the school paper, and came to know the real plight of his native country. His first work, *Spirits Rebellious*, attacked oppression, tyranny, and various customs of the land....

He considered himself a kind of "prophet," with a special mission to speak up for the masses and liberate them from the various evils that had befallen them as a result of their inertia, customs and traditions. Had the

Ottoman authorities been less ruthless, we would probably have seen Gibran leading demonstrations, and writings in the local press to awaken a social consciousness in the minds of his countrymen....

Family problems brought Gibran back to the United States, where he continued to paint and write. He spent some time in Paris studying art. Later he opened a studio in New York, where he painted much and wrote most of his works.

His untimely death came on April 10, 1931, while he was at the peak of his powers. Gibran was then forty-eight. After much respect was paid to his remains in the United States, the coffin draped in the Stars and Stripes and the Lebanese flag was taken to Lebanon aboard the ship *Providence*. The reception given in his native land was unprecedented.... To this day, people visit his tomb as a place of pilgrimage. Even after his death, Gibran continued to be a paradoxical figure to the readers.

Andrew Sherfan

Your friend is your needs answered.
   He is your field which you sow with love
   and reap with thanksgiving.
   ...you come to him with your hunger,
   and you seek him for peace.
   And let there be no purpose in friendship
   save the deepening of the spirit.

The power to
Love is God's greatest gift to man,
For it never will be taken from the
Blessed one who loves.

Your most radiant garment
   is of the other person's weaving;
   Your most savory meal
   is that which you eat at the other person's table;
   Your most comfortable bed
   is in the other person's house.
   Now tell me, how can you separate yourself
   from the other person?

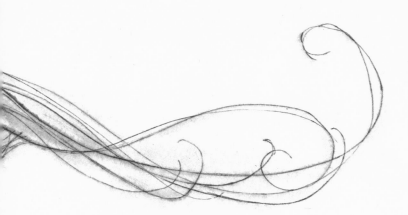

From a sensitive woman's heart
  springs the happiness of mankind,
  and from the kindness of her noble spirit
comes mankind's affection.

I believe that it is in you to be good citizens.
    And what is it to be a good citizen?
    It is to acknowledge the other person's rights
before asserting your own,
but always to be conscious of your own.
    It is to be free in word and deed,
but it is also to know that your freedom
is subject to the other person's freedom.
    It is to create the useful and the beautiful
with your own hands, and to admire
what others have created in love and with faith.

Truth is a deep kindness that teaches us
to be content with our everyday life
and share with the people the same happiness.

We are friends....
I want nothing from you,
and you want nothing from me.
We share life.

The song of the voice is sweet,
but the song of the heart
is the pure voice of heaven.

Heaven fills my lamp with oil
and I place it at my window
to direct the Stranger through the dark.
I do all these things
because I live in them....
For I am a poet, and if I cannot give,
I shall refuse to receive.

My brothers, seek counsel of one another,
    for therein lies the way
    out of error and futile repentance.
    The wisdom of the many
    is your shield against tyranny.
    For when we turn to one another for counsel
    we reduce the number of our enemies.

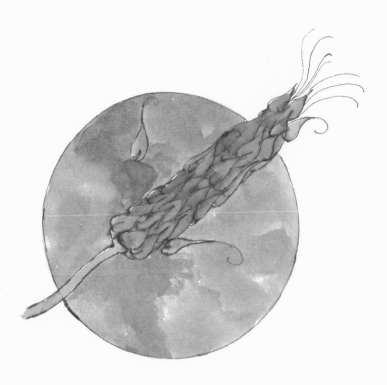

Generosity is not in giving me that
which I need more than you do,
but it is in giving me that
which you need more than I do.

We seek one another in our aloneness,
   and we walk the road
   when we have no hearth to sit beside.
   My friends and my brothers,
   the wider road is your fellowman.

When you tell your trouble to your neighbor
you present him with a part of your heart.
If he possesses a great soul,
he thanks you....

Darkness may hide the trees
    and the flowers from the eyes
    but it cannot hide love
    from the soul.

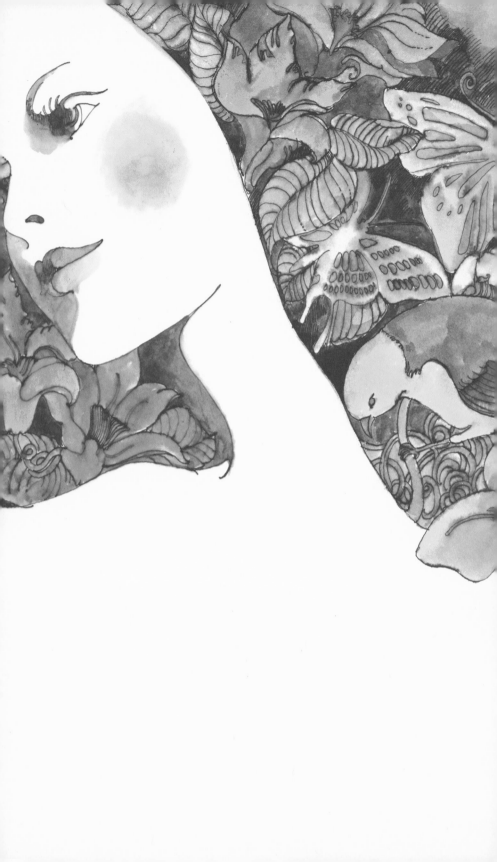

Beauty is that which attracts your soul,
    and that which loves to give
    and not to receive.
    When you meet Beauty, you feel
    that the hands deep within your inner self
    are stretched forth to bring her
    into the domain of your heart.

You and I are all children of one faith,
   for the divers paths of religion are fingers
   of the loving hand of one Supreme Being,
   a hand extended to all, offering completeness
   of spirit to all, eager to receive all.

The sympathy that touches the neighbour's heart
is more supreme than the hidden virtue
in the unseen corners of the convent.

Love, take me.
  Take me, Beauty.
  Take me, Earth.
  I take you,
  Love, Earth, Beauty.
  I take
  God.

The coin which you drop into
   The withered hand stretching toward
You is the only golden chain that
Binds your rich heart to the
Loving heart of God....

Your inner soul, my friend, is surrounded
  with solitude and seclusion.
  Were it not for this solitude and this seclusion
  you would not be you and I would not be I.
  If it were not for that solitude and seclusion,
  I would, if I heard your voice,
  think myself to be speaking;
  yet, if I saw your face, I would imagine
  that I were looking into a mirror.

Love lies in the soul alone,
    Not in the body, and like wine
Should stimulate our better self
    To welcome gifts of Love Divine.

If we were to do away with the various religions,
   we would find ourselves united
   and enjoying one great faith and religion,
   abounding in brotherhood.

The flowers of the field are the children
   of sun's affection and nature's love;
   and the children of men are the flowers
   of love and compassion.

I love you, my brother, whoever you are—
whether you worship in your church,
kneel in your temple, or pray in your mosque.

We live upon one another according to the law,
ancient and timeless.
Let us live thus in loving-kindness.

God created music
as a common language for all men.
It inspires the poets,
the composers and the architects.
It lures us to search our souls
for the meaning of the mysteries
described in ancient books.

Humanity is the spirit
of the Supreme Being on earth,
and that Supreme Being
preaches love and good will.

He who understands you
    is greater kin to you
    than your own brother.
    For even your own kindred
    may neither understand you
    nor know your true worth.

The heart's affections are divided
like the branches of the cedar tree;
if the tree loses one strong branch,
it will suffer but it does not die.
It will pour all its vitality
into the next branch so that it will grow
and fill the empty place.

Set in Romanee, a twentieth-century typeface
designed by Jan van Krimpen of Holland.
Printed on Hallmark Ivory Vellux.
Designed by Rainer K. Koenig.